THE QUIET WAYS HE LOVED

Verses Kindler Publication

Verses Kindler Publication.
Website: www.verseskindlerpublication.com

The Quiet Ways He Loved
By: Sushma Nalluri
ISBN: 978-93-47494-59-8
1st Edition
Price: INR 199/$13

Disclaimer

The Quiet Ways He Loved *is* authored by Sushma Nalluri. The entirety of this published work comprises the original content of the author, who has undertaken diligent efforts in its editing. The characters depicted herein may be fictitious or inspired by real events; however, they are not intended to cause offense or represent any prejudice against any caste or system. Any similarity to the names of actual individuals, locations, or institutions is purely coincidental and serves the narrative. The author bears sole responsibility for the originality of this work; the publisher assumes no liability thereof.

Table of Contents

Dedication

To all the fathers who love quietly and protect without making it obvious. To the men who stand steady like lighthouses, never asking to be noticed, yet always ensuring the way ahead is safe.

To those who turn "I care" into everyday actions; remembering the smallest preferences, checking in without being asked, standing beside us during difficult days, thinking two steps ahead so we wouldn't have to, and packing something extra 'just in case'.

You may call it responsibility. You may call it ordinary.

But to us, it was strength. It was safety. It was the steady light that quietly shaped us and gave us the courage to grow.

Author's Note

Most of the time, we don't realise we are being shaped. We think we are just eating breakfast, walking to the car, or arguing about which film to watch. We assume these are ordinary days passing by.

These pages are about those ordinary days.

I did not begin this narrative to write about a grand hero. What unfolded instead were these memories: small, steady moments that quietly built a life. A father's *(Nanna in Telugu)* hand resting on a shoulder. A routine repeated without announcement. A short sentence that carried more meaning than it seemed to.

I was never given any formal lectures at home or long speeches about values. My learning happened in simple ways; while travelling together, while reading the news, while sitting in the same room. I understood the world by observing how he responded to it; how he listened carefully, how he stayed calm, how he chose his words.

These reflections are arranged as they came to me, beginning from the years when I was small enough to stand beside him and reach only his waist, and moving into the time when I slowly began making decisions on my own. Nothing here has been polished to sound grand. A shared meal is simply a meal. A small reminder is just that. But repeated over the years, such moments begin to shape who we become.

This account is not meant to glorify a person. It is an attempt to understand what a steady presence can do in a life. It is about how habits are absorbed quietly: the way we speak, the way we think, the way we handle difficulty, without ever realising we are learning.

As you move through these pages, you may recognise something from your own home. A routine. A familiar phrase. A small habit you once thought was insignificant.

We rarely recognise the moments that shape us while we are living them. They don't arrive with applause or warning. They settle in quietly, through small, repeated actions, everyday consistency, and care that exists without seeking credit. What feels ordinary in the moment often becomes the architecture of who we are becoming.

These memories are my way of understanding how those simple days shaped me.

1
Small Acts, Steady Love

From the beginning, people spoke about my eyes. Relatives would sit on our sofa, sip their tea, and lean over my cradle. "Same eyes as her father," they would say. My eyes were brown, but they shifted toward hazel in different light. In the balcony sunlight, they appeared lighter; in the hallway, deeper and steadier. Amma would repeat the comment to him in the evening. He would look at me quietly for a few seconds and say one word. "Same."

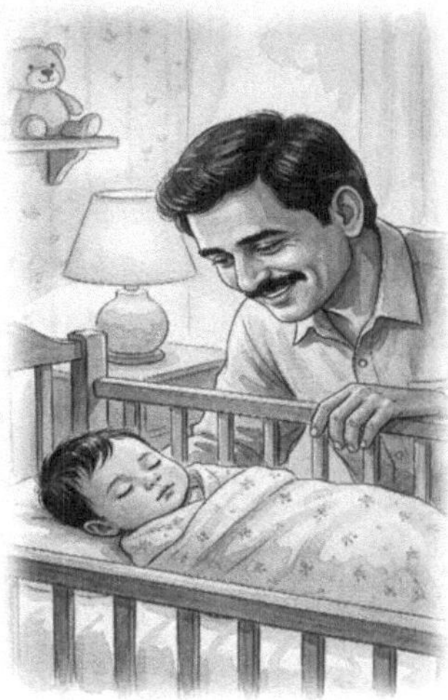

He was extremely happy that I looked like him. He did not express it loudly. It showed in the way he kept looking at me in those early months; not dramatically, just steadily. Amma said he became a different person after we were born. First my elder brother, then me. She said something shifted in him. Not suddenly. Steadily.

Before having children, he was focused on studies and his career. He had completed an MA in English, a Master's in Law, and an MA in Islamic Studies. At that time, no one else in his family was educated at that level. He studied independently without guidance. He deeply respected books and knowledge. He believed knowledge protects from unexpected situations. "Education will stand by you," he would say later, folding the newspaper carefully after reading it.

By the time I was born, he was teaching in a law college and practising as a lawyer in court. His days were divided between classrooms and courtrooms. Blackboards and legal briefs. But once we came into his life, his focus widened. Education was no longer only his personal achievement. It became something he wanted to build for us. Along with that came something else: watchfulness.

He became more careful about everyday details. He checked window latches at night. He warned us about damp floors. He adjusted the ceiling fan if it made even a slight sound. He noticed furniture corners and loose wires. At that time, it felt normal. Only much later did I understand that these small checks were his quiet way of building safety around us.

When my first birthday approached in 2002, that same attentiveness showed itself in a different form. He became particular about one thing: the cake. He did not want a round cake. He wanted a heart-shaped one.

At that time, heart-shaped cakes were not common in our town. Most bakeries displayed round cakes with thick white cream and bright cherries. Some made square cakes for larger gatherings. When he asked, "Do you have a heart-shaped cake?" most shopkeepers shook their heads. One even suggested buying a round cake and adjusting it at home. He did not agree. He wanted the shape to be right from the beginning.

He found a small bakery willing to prepare it if he waited. He waited. On the evening of my birthday, the heart-shaped cake sat in the middle of our hall on a small steel table. The table was light and slightly uneven, the kind that made a faint humming sound if someone shifted their weight against it. Amma had covered it with a blue cloth, tucking the edges neatly underneath so the legs wouldn't show.

The cake itself was simple. A white cream base. A blue border made of small piped stars. My name was written in red icing that looked slightly glossy under the tube light. If you looked closely at the photograph now, one curve of the heart was a little uneven. It was not perfectly symmetrical. But it was clearly a heart.

I was sitting in front of it in that photograph. The frock I wore looked slightly larger than me. My elder brother stood beside me, leaning forward, watching the cake as if calculating when he might get his piece. Nanna stood behind me, one hand steadying my back so I did not fall from the chair.

The house was full that evening. Family members from nearby towns. Neighbours from down the street. Children running through the rooms. Steel plates were stacked on the dining table.

He placed the cake on the steel table himself. He steadied my hand before I touched the knife.

He clicked many pictures that day, not only the main cake-cutting moment. He captured the seconds in between. I stared at the candle flame. My brother was whispering something. Amma was fixing my dress. An aunt was feeding me a small bit of icing. At that time, cameras required planning. You had to buy film rolls. You had only thirty-six exposures. Each click had to matter. He developed every roll. He arranged the prints carefully in albums. He labelled them neatly. He kept them safe.

That habit of keeping things safe did not stop with photographs. In our house, there was a suitcase where he stored small things connected to us. School crafts made of coloured paper. Certificates. Old notebooks. Progress reports. Years later, I found my first drawing inside it: a sun in one corner, a river, mountains in the background, a small house placed carefully in the middle, and clouds drifting above. The lines were uneven. The colours did not stay within the borders. He had kept it for twenty-one years. Next to it were my brother's report cards from Class 9 and 10, every teacher's remark preserved.

I had forgotten that drawing existed. He had not.

Keeping things safe was instinctive for him; not because they were important for the future, but because they were memories he wanted to treasure.

Around the same time, another routine quietly became part of our lives. Temple visits grew regular.

One fine day, he took our whole family to Tirupati. The lines were long. The corridors narrow. The air was warm and heavy. He carried me so I would not get pushed. His other hand rested firmly on my brother's shoulder. After darshan, he made sure we sat somewhere calm before leaving.

Similarly, he also took us to Srikalahasti and to other temples. The purpose was clear to him: blessings and protection from the evil eye. At Srikalahasti, he stood patiently during the ceremony. He listened carefully to the priest. He ensured the sacred threads were tied firmly around our wrists. He checked the knots himself. He made sure we received prasad properly before stepping outside. He believed rituals should be done properly. Not hurried. Not carelessly.

Temple visits slowly became a regular habit, especially on Saturdays. Growing up, he would take me to the Venkateswara Swamy temple. To ring the temple bell, he would lift me up. The rope felt rough in my hand. The bell would echo loudly. After aarti, he would gently place the warmth of the flame near my eyes. "Close your eyes," he would say softly. He made sure I did not miss any blessings. Maybe this is how many of us have rung temple bells — lifted up by someone taller, held steady for a moment, and told to close our eyes before the warmth of the flame. Do you remember this scenario from your childhood?

Whether he was lifting me toward the temple bell or calmly brushing away an admiring glance, the instinct behind both felt the same.

Whenever someone praised me, his reaction came naturally. If a neighbour said, "She looks so beautiful," or "Look at those eyes," his hand would move in a small circle over my head. He would flick his fingers lightly, as if brushing something away. He did not interrupt the conversation. He did not explain the gesture. He just did it.

As a child, I assumed every father did this.

Looking back now, I saw that the same man who believed knowledge protects from unexpected situations also believed blessings matter. Law books and temple threads existed side by side in our home. Education and rituals were not opposites for him. They were both forms of protection.

When someone once said, "She looks exactly like you," he replied quietly, "Let her be better." It was not dramatic. It was steady.

When I looked again at that heart-shaped cake photograph, I noticed more than the cake. I noticed the way he bent down to our height. I noticed his hand near my shoulder. I noticed how present he was in that frame.

At that time, I only saw a birthday. Now I see a man who had already changed in serene ways; a man who showed love not through big declarations, but through repetition, through care taken seriously, through a cake shaped like a heart when round ones were easier, through photographs labelled neatly, through sacred threads tied firmly, and through small circles drawn in the air to keep something unseen away from his child.

Small acts, done consistently, became the steady love that shaped the beginning of my life.

* * *

If I were to hold those years in a few lines, they would sound like this.

He did not speak in grand displays,

He stood beside me through my days.

In small acts, in steady love,

He stayed close enough.

Before you turn the page:

Picture one room from your childhood, notice who is standing nearest to you, and stay with that moment for a while. Note how you feel about it.

2

Routines That Stayed

By the time I turned three, mornings had already begun to belong to Nanna. He would wake up before sunrise, when the air outside still carried a mild chill, and the streets were quieter than usual. I did not know what discipline meant, but I knew that if he stepped out, I wanted to go with him. That was how my daily exercise routine began. I would walk beside him, sometimes holding his finger, sometimes trying to match his pace. My steps were small and uneven. He adjusted without saying so.

He had been a national athlete in his younger years and remained deeply connected to sports for a long time. I later learned that in his twenties, before marriage, he was the only person from Andhra Pradesh selected to take part in the Republic Day Parade in Delhi. Around the same time, he was also selected for the Indian Army, but he chose to return home and prepare for the Civil Services instead, studying alongside his law degree. Though the path did not ultimately lead him there, he never stopped learning. His discipline showed in his body too—sprint runs and long runs, swimming, javelin throw, shot put; he had done it all.

As a child, I did not fully understand what any of this meant. I only knew he stretched with precision and moved with ease. He never announced that I should exercise. He never said, "This will help you later." He simply let me stand beside him while he bent, stretched, and counted softly under his breath. Sometimes he would show me how to touch my toes. Sometimes he would clap once and say, "Run till that pole and come back." I would run halfway and turn around. He would pretend it was enough.

Those mornings were not dramatic. There were no speeches about fitness. Just repetition. His steady rhythm. My smaller rhythm is slowly learning to follow. It became normal for me to wake up early. It became normal to move before the day began. I did not know then that a habit was forming. I only knew that I liked being near him.

Evenings had a different energy. That was when our movie routine began. Nanna liked taking the whole family to the theatre. He enjoyed the outing as much as the film itself. The smell of popcorn, the dim lights, the large screen; it all felt important to me. But I was too young for certain scenes. Whenever an action sequence began and the volume suddenly rose, I would panic. I remember burying my face in Amma's saree or clutching Nanna's arm tightly.

"It's just a movie," he would say quietly.

He never laughed at me. He never told me to stop crying. Amma would pat my back. Sometimes he would gently cover my ears until the noise settled. Gradually, I began lifting my head and watching again. Slowly, the fear reduced. Not because the scenes changed, but because I felt safe enough to look.

During festivals, movie-watching moved from theatres to our living rooms. We would sit together, eat together, and watch whatever special films were telecast on television. Those evenings were simple. Plates on the floor. The ceiling fan hummed above us. Nanna leaned back against the wall. I did not realise it then, but this was how he taught us to be together.

He preferred old movies. "These are better," he would insist. He introduced us to Alluri Sitaramaraju, Lava Kusa, Mayabazar, and Tenali Ramakrishna. He would explain small details while watching.

"See how they speak," he would say. "See the values."

At that time, I was not very interested. The pace felt slow to me. The songs were longer than I liked. But he watched patiently. He also played old songs from the 90s. He said they were peaceful. I remember thinking they were too calm. Now, when I hear those songs, I understand what he meant.

Looking back, I see that he was not forcing preferences. He was quietly sharing his world with us.

When I turned four, Saturdays found a new meaning. We began visiting the Venkateswara Swamy temple regularly. Every family has a day they keep for something sacred. For us, it was Saturday. The temple stood steady, its stone floors cool even in summer. The air carried the smell of camphor and jasmine. The bell hung high above.

To ring it, I had to be lifted. Nanna would hold me firmly and raise me just enough so my fingers could reach the rope. It felt rough in my palm. I would pull it down with effort. The bell would echo loudly across the temple courtyard. That sound felt powerful. I did not know why.

Temple visits became part of our weekly rhythm. We did not debate faith. We simply showed up. We stood in line. We received prasad. We walked back home.

By the time I entered first and second class, books had quietly become part of our home environment. They were everywhere. Law books were stacked neatly. Literature filled the shelves. Newspapers were folded and placed in order. Nanna believed deeply that knowledge protects us from unexpected situations. He did not separate subjects.

"Read anything," he would say. "Stories, novels, GK books. Just read."

When I had to attend my friends' birthdays, he would sometimes bring GK books as gifts. I did not always appreciate that choice. I thought toys would be more exciting. But he remained consistent. For him, a book was always valuable. He liked the feel of hard copies.

"When you hold a book, you remember better," he would say.

He encouraged underlining important lines. Highlighting. Turning pages slowly.

Gradually, I began reading on my own. At first, to show him that I had read something. Later, as I began enjoying it, current affairs began to make sense. I noticed that conversations at home felt different when I had read something beforehand. I could respond. I could ask questions. Without announcing it, he had built another habit into my life.

Temple on Saturdays. Books during the week. Exercise in the mornings. Movies in the evenings. Quiet patterns were forming.

During the second class, there was one incident that showed me another side of him. Our school took us on a trip to Manasarovar, about 40 kilometres from our town. We had water activities and ground games. I enjoyed it so much that the very next day I wanted to go again.

It was a half-day at school. I came home and insisted.

"Take me," I said repeatedly.

He told me it might be closed by the time we reached. It usually shuts by five in the evening. He explained calmly. I did not listen. I was stubborn. I kept asking.

He was busy that day. Even now, I remember that he had work. But after hearing me insist several times, he agreed. Amma packed dosas, almost as if she knew how it would unfold.

By the time we reached, it was around four in the evening. The water rides were closed. The ground rides were shutting down exactly as he had predicted.

He did not say, "I told you."

He did not show irritation.

He did not mention wasted time.

Instead, we walked around the area. We found a swing that was still open. I played. He watched. We sat down and ate the dosas Amma had packed. He fed me patiently, tearing off pieces and handing them to me. The sun was lowering slightly. The place was quieter than the previous day.

It was not the grand outing I had imagined. But it was peaceful.

At that age, I did not analyse his response. I simply felt satisfied that he had come with me. Now, I understand something elsc. He chose patience over correction. He chose my happiness over convenience.

Those years from three to six were not dramatic. There were no life-changing speeches. There were no big achicvements. But if I look closely, I see how carefully he was building me.

Body through exercise.

Emotion through safety during movies.

Belief through temple rituals.

Protection through small hand gestures.

Knowledge through books.

Character through patience.

None of it was explained formally. It was lived daily.

When I think of those mornings when he slowed his pace for my small steps, or those evenings when he covered my ears during loud scenes, or those Saturdays when he lifted me to ring a bell that felt too high, I see consistency more than intensity.

He did not declare love loudly. He practised it quietly.

I did not realise then how dependent I was on those routines. They felt ordinary. They were anything but.

And somewhere between a temple bell, a GK book, and a dosa eaten outside closed rides, I was growing; shaped by repetition, steadiness, and a father who never needed applause to do what he believed was right.

* * *

That was the rhythm of those days.

He matched his steps to mine,

He steadied what I feared.

In days that looked ordinary,

He built the routines that stayed.

Before you turn the page:

Notice which routines shaped you, and who stood behind them. You'll find yourself smiling for sure.

3

The Night the Fever Rose

The routines from those years had settled into our lives so naturally that none of us expected interruption. Saturday temple visits, evening reading, ordinary school days—everything moved in a steady rhythm. One of my strongest memories from those years is learning to ride a bicycle. Nanna bought me a Ladybird cycle soon after it had launched. To me, it looked enormous. Since I was still small, he fixed the supporting side wheels so I could balance. Every morning, he would walk beside me as I tried to pedal, steadying the handle whenever it tilted too much. Slowly, the wobble disappeared. One day, the side wheels were no longer needed.

Then, on a rainy week, I developed a fever. At first, it seemed simple. I vomit and felt unusually cold even when the air was warm. Amma touched my forehead and immediately slipped into the efficiency with which she handled anything concerning our well-being. Over the next few days, she kept a close eye on me; bringing lime juice, buttermilk or coconut water, making sure I ate properly, and checking in whenever she could. I believed her when she said it would settle, and for a few days, I even continued going to school, trusting the steady care that surrounded me.

But the temperature did not settle. It climbed sheepishly. One evening it was 100. Then 101. Then 102. I remember lying in bed, shivering, though sweat covered my skin. Doctors said it could be viral fever or maybe malaria. Dengue was not clearly understood in our town then. Tablets were prescribed. Amma brought buttermilk and light food. Nanna sat beside me through the night, adjusting the sheet when I kicked it away. His presence felt normal. I did not yet realise he was measuring every temperature rise.

When the fever reached 104°C, the mood in the house changed. We went out again late at night. I sat between Amma and Nanna on the bike, my head resting against his back. The road was nearly empty. Streetlights passed in intervals. At the clinic, blood tests were done. We waited longer than usual. When the results came in, I heard one number repeated softly: platelets had dropped to around 40,000. I did not understand what that meant. I only noticed Amma's eyes filling with tears.

Blood was injected there, but it did not improve my condition enough. The doctors felt I would need better treatment elsewhere. The fever was still high, and arrangements had to be made quickly. But Amma and Nanna did not let me feel the seriousness of it. They simply told me we were going somewhere else for a few days. That same night, we boarded a train to Hyderabad. I remember being wrapped in a shawl, half-awake, hearing station announcements echo in the dark. Nanna did not discuss things loudly. He simply acted.

We reached Rainbow Hospital in Jubilee Hills. It was expensive for us at that time, though I learned that later. At the hospital, doctors examined my reports and said the platelet injection was urgent. The situation was critical. One of Nanna's friends donated blood without hesitation. Platelets were arranged and injected. I lay on the hospital bed, watching nurses come and go. I did not fully grasp the seriousness of it. I only knew my parents were close.

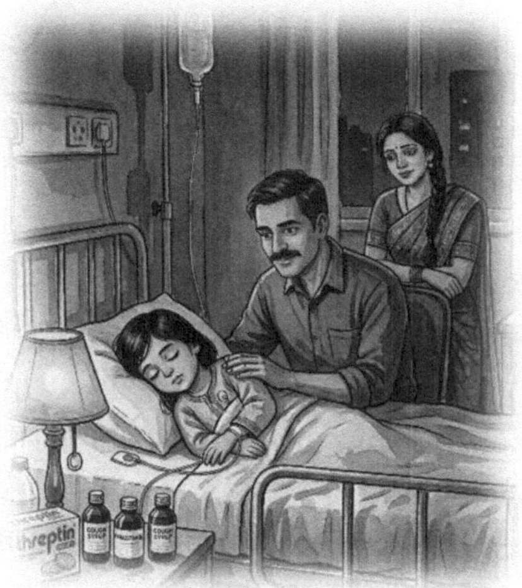

I stayed in the hospital for almost five days. Nanna remained beside me almost continuously. If I opened my eyes at night, he was sitting there. He bought fruits, healthy food, and Treptin biscuits. From that time on, Treptin became a regular biscuit in our house. "Eat one more," he would say gently, as if it were medicine. He talked to me, adjusted my pillow, and sometimes tried to distract me with small stories. Amma moved between prayer and practical tasks, making sure I was comfortable.

Later, Amma told me that she had seen Nanna cry once in front of the doctor when my condition was at its worst. I never saw him cry. To me, he remained steady. Amma also made a devoted vow to take me to Tirupati once I recovered. None of this was dramatic in the moment. It unfolded in hospital corridors and silent waiting rooms. The unplanned expenses were heavy, but Nanna managed them without speaking about the strain in front of me. He kept that weight separate from my bed.

Little by little, when my fever reduced, and my strength began to return, we came back home. Discharge felt simple. There was no celebration, just relief. Recovery took time. I returned to school gradually. I was weaker, but I was present. The world outside had not changed much; classes continued, homework resumed, and friends asked why I had been absent. I answered lightly. Inside, I was still adjusting to normalcy.

As my health improved, our home settled back into its familiar rhythm. Recovery was not hurried. Amma made sure I took my medicines on time and watched over the small routines of healing with patience. Nanna returned from outside carrying things he believed would help me regain strength: fruits, Treptin biscuits, and other nourishing foods. Food in our home was never random. Amma and Nanna were both very conscious about health. Whenever they gave us something to eat, they would explain why it mattered; how fruits helped the body recover, why certain foods strengthened us, and why balanced food kept us well. Those meaningful and much-needed explanations stayed with me. My parents created a steady circle of care around me, making sure I rested, ate well, and gradually found my energy again.

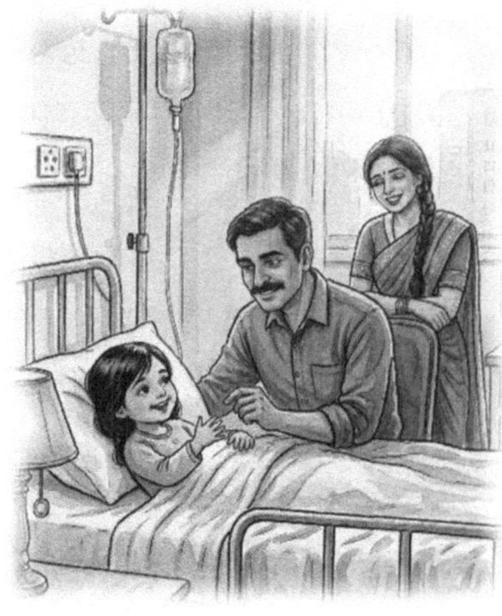

During those quieter days of recovery, I spent more time

sitting with books. What began as a way to pass the long, restful hours slowly turned into something deeper. Page by page, books opened small windows to the world beyond my room; stories, ideas, and questions that stayed with me long after I closed them. Without realising it then, that companionship with books began shaping a curiosity that continues to guide and inspire me even now.

GK reading slowly became a habit. Current affairs began to interest me. Conversations at home included small discussions about news or facts I had read. Nanna had studied at Osmania College in Hyderabad, where he had learned Hindi well. Sometimes at home, he would switch languages while speaking with me. A conversation that began in English would suddenly continue in Hindi and then return to English again. At the time, it felt like an easy and unimportant game, but gradually it helped me become comfortable speaking both languages. It was never forced. It happened naturally over dinner or in the evening. After experiencing such physical weakness, strengthening my mind felt steady. I did not think of it as recovery at the time. It was simply the next step.

Looking back, I see how those days carried two forms of care. One was urgent and decisive; late-night doctor visits, train journeys, hospital admissions, platelet injections arranged without delay. The other was quiet and consistent; biscuits brought daily, a chair kept close to the bed, a vow made silently, expenses handled without complaint. Both existed side by side.

The routines from earlier years did not disappear. They resumed. Temple visits continued. Often after the temple visit, we would step out for a small treat. There was a place that was quite popular in those days, where we would sit together and talk while I happily ate chaat or pani puri or whatever I liked that evening. It became our Saturday ritual. School activities picked up. School projects also started becoming part of those years. Amma carefully supervised my studies and homework. Nanna would step in whenever something needed extra effort outside the textbooks. For speeches, debates, and elocution competitions, we did not have the internet then. Nanna became my search engine. He would help me gather information, shape the ideas, and make the content clearer before I presented it in school. Additionally, reading deepened. At the time, it did not feel like a change worth noticing. It was simply part of the days I was living through. Much later, I recognised that the steadiness I carried through both difficult moments and ordinary days had been shaped quietly during those years.

When I think of that time now, I do not first remember fear. I remember the feel of sitting between my parents on a bike at night. I remember hospital lights, Treptin biscuits placed near my pillow, and Nanna's voice asking, "Are you okay?" I remember returning home and opening a book again. Life did not announce its recovery. It returned quietly.

The fever rose, but so did something else: a deeper awareness of how closely I was held.

* * *

When I think of those hospital days, this is what remains.

The night the fever rose,

When the fever tested us,

He did not raise his voice or show fear.

Between trains, drips, and waiting rooms,

He chose to remain steady and near.

Before you turn the page:

A child may forget the fever. But somewhere in memory remains the person who stayed awake through the night so the child could sleep. Take a minute and recall who kept that silent watch for you.

4

Framed in Pride

Childhood achievements are often small things: drawings, certificates, a few careful lines on paper. At that age, they rarely feel significant. Yet sometimes a parent's response gives those small efforts a life far beyond the moment. The national flag I drew in fourth class was done on a plain white sheet that curled slightly at the edges once the sketch pens dried. I remember sitting at the table, carefully outlining the Ashoka Chakra, counting the spokes twice so I would not make a mistake. When I finished, I showed it to Nanna without thinking much about it. He held the paper steady, looked at it for a few quiet seconds, and said, "You have drawn it properly." A week later, I walked into his office and saw it framed and hung on the wall behind his table, beside his book racks. It was placed where every client could see it. When people asked about it, he would say, "My daughter drew that." He did not say it loudly, but his smile when he said it stayed with me. He celebrated small things as if they were important milestones. He treated my simple drawing like something worthy of preservation.

After I recovered from dengue, Amma fulfilled the vow she had made to take me to Tirupati. We travelled there as a family. The temple corridors were crowded, and the queue moved slowly, but Nanna stood patiently. After darshan, he ensured we received prasad properly and asked me to stand still for a moment before the idol. From Tirupati, we travelled to Chennai and then to Kanchipuram. The trip combined temple visits and time in different surroundings, which had become our usual pattern. I preferred natural places and open landscapes, but he insisted that temples mattered just as much. Nanna would point to carvings on pillars and speak about architecture and history in simple words. He explained the presence of the idol and how people found peace standing before it. He believed faith existed in small acts such as ringing the bell with attention, tying a thread with intention, and receiving prasad respectfully. At that age, I listened without fully understanding, but Nanna continued explaining with ease and calmness.

Growing up, many of our trips followed this rhythm. There would be a temple first and then time in nature. I would often suggest waterfalls or hills, and he would agree, but only after visiting a temple nearby. Nanna firmly believed understanding the history and structure of a temple gave depth to a journey. He would ask me to observe the carvings, the symmetry of pillars, and the stillness inside the sanctum. Even when I was impatient, he remained steady. Those repeated visits slowly shaped how I began to look at places. Even if I did not admit it then, something inside me was learning to pause.

Around the age of ten, sports became more structured in my routine. Exercise had been part of my life since childhood, and those early morning habits supported what came next. Nanna, being a national athlete, had strong knowledge of sports and discipline. He introduced me to tennis coaching, and over time, I began attending regularly. The court felt unfamiliar in the beginning, and the racket seemed heavier than I expected. He often stood near the fence, observing quietly. His instructions were brief and simple. “Move your feet first.” “Watch the ball carefully.”

At home, sports also became something we shared in quieter ways. Nanna loved watching cricket, and we would often sit together during matches. I did not have much knowledge of the game then, but he would explain what was happening on the field; why a particular shot was good, why a bowler changed pace, or why field placements mattered. Sometimes he would pause and ask, “What do you think will happen next?” I rarely had the right answer, but he listened patiently anyway. Slowly, the game began to make sense, and those conversations became something I looked forward to.

Because exercise had already built basic stamina, I adjusted gradually. Tennis practice became consistent, and my health and stamina improved steadily. His spirit influenced the way I approached practice. He treated sport as a habit, not an excitement. That early discipline later became the foundation for my competitive participation in sports.

Simultaneously, school competitions increased during this period as well. I began participating more actively in elocution, writing competitions, quizzes, debates, and anchoring school events. Participation had begun from my early school years, but during this time, my confidence grew visibly. Whenever I returned home with a certificate, he would read it carefully. If I won, he shared the news proudly with relatives and friends, speaking about it as though it were his own achievement. If I did not win, he would say, "Next time, participate again." He encouraged me to raise my hand without hesitation. Participation mattered more than the result.

Around this time, he also bought me a small whiteboard for my room. His idea was simple: I could write down lessons, ideas, or anything important I was learning so that it would stay in my mind more clearly. I began using it to practice speeches, take notes for competitions, and revise things I wanted to remember. It became a small space where I could organise my thoughts before presenting them.

I remember rehearsing for a debate and speaking too quickly. He listened and said, "Slow down so they understand you." The next day, I remembered his advice on stage. Afterwards, he simply said, "You were clear." That was enough.

Those years moved with a steady pace. A drawing framed in an office. A vow fulfilled at Tirupati. Trips to Chennai and Kanchi. Temple bells and sacred threads. Tennis practice under the sun. Certificates were placed carefully on a table. Growth unfurled without noise.

Nanna did not announce pride; he expressed it through small gestures that stayed with me. Nanna never spoke at length about discipline, yet he was always present for it; in temple visits, in early practice sessions, in listening to a speech rehearsal, or reading a certificate with calm attention. Through temples, sports, and competitions, Nanna devised an environment where effort felt natural, and confidence grew without hesitation.

* * *

If I were to gather those growing years into modest expression, they might sound like:

Framed in pride, a simple drawing earned its place,

On an office wall, in steady sight, not hidden out of grace.

Between temple bells and tennis courts, small efforts grew inside,

And in each quiet celebration, my courage learned to stride.

Before you turn the page:

A child may forget the drawing or the medal. But they rarely forget the person who treated it like something precious. As you read these pages, you may have remembered small moments from your own childhood—times when someone noticed your effort and made it feel important.

Who is the first person that comes to your mind?

5

The Smile That Meant Everything

Life slowly began to take on a different rhythm as I grew older. It's funny how that happens; one day you're colouring apples and playing hopscotch without a care in the world, and the next, the stakes feel just a little bit higher. School was no longer just about classes and routine days. Activities, competitions, and small achievements started filling my time. I began participating in many events: elocution, writing competitions, quizzes, debates, and even anchoring school programs.

I did not think too much about what these moments meant then. For me, they were simply prospects to try something new and enjoy being involved. Have you ever wondered if those "just for fun" moments were actually the building blocks of who you are today?

In retrospect, elocution wasn't just about speaking; it was about finding my voice. Quizzing wasn't just about facts; it was about curiosity. But behind every small step I took, there was always one presence watching with steady attention. Nanna never pushed me forcefully toward any activity, yet his encouragement was always there. If there were an event, he would say, "You should try." That was enough.

Whenever I returned home after participating in something at school, he would ask how it went. Sometimes I would describe everything in detail, usually when I was buzzing with that "I actually did it!" energy; sometimes I would give a short answer and move on. But he always listened carefully. What I noticed more clearly was the way he spoke about my participation to others. When he met his friends or spoke with family members, he would mention these small moments as if they were something worth sharing. There was a certain happiness in his expression when he spoke about it. He never exaggerated or praised loudly. It was just a calm sentence and a smile. At that time, I did not think of it as pride. It felt normal. Isn't it strange how we often mistake a parent's deepest support for "just the way things are" until we're older? Now, I acknowledge how much those moments meant to him.

Sports had always been present in our home. As mentioned earlier, my father had been a national athlete, so physical activity was something he naturally valued. From the beginning, Nanna and I often exercised together; sometimes jogging in the mornings, sometimes sprinting short distances. At that age, it did not feel like training. Staying active became part of our routine. There was never any pressure attached to it. It was absolutely something we did together. Over time, I started learning different sports. Tennis came first, and later I began playing shuttle as well. Nanna knew a great deal about sports, and like most fathers, he shared that knowledge casually, never making it feel like a formal lesson. Small corrections, advice, and encouragement gradually shaped how I approached these activities. Those early habits of running and staying active later became the quiet foundation for the competitions I would take part in during my school years.

My involvement in school competitions continued. I participated in different events and gradually started doing well in them. Whenever something went well, my father's reaction remained simple but meaningful. He would listen, smile, and sometimes share the moment with others. That pride stayed with me more than any trophy or certificate. What I also began noticing was how smoothly he balanced encouragement with calmness. There was never an overwhelming sense of excitement, and there was never disappointment if something did not go as planned. His response was always steady. It created a space where trying felt more important than winning. In a world that constantly demands "the best," how often do we actually get the grace to "try"?

One of the routines I remember most clearly from those years was our walks together. Whenever we walked side by side, I would hold him around the waist while he placed his arm gently over my shoulder. It was a small gesture, but it always made me feel safe. Those walks were never meant to be serious conversations. They happened. As we moved through the streets, he would talk about different situations he had seen during his work. Being an advocate meant he came across many kinds of people and experienced every day. Instead of keeping those things separate from family life, he would share them simply and in a friendly way.

Through those conversations, he slowly introduced me to the realities of the outside world. He would explain how people behave, how situations can change quickly, and why it is important to observe before reacting. He never spoke in a way that sounded like a lecture. It felt more like two friends discussing things that had happened during the day. Sometimes he would ask what I thought about a situation, making me feel like my opinion actually carried weight, and then he would add his perspective. These dialogues did not feel like lessons at the time. But over the years, they shaped the way I understand people and situations.

Because of these exchanges, I developed a certain instinct about the world around me. I learned to notice small details in behaviour and intentions. I learned how to stay aware without becoming fearful. Most importantly, I learned how to behave with respect while still protecting myself. These ideas were never presented as rules, but were made a part of our everyday conversations as we walked together. Have you ever looked back and realised someone was preparing you for a battle you didn't even know you'd have to fight? Looking back, I realise how carefully he was preparing me to face the world on my own someday, without ever making it feel like preparation.

Sports gradually became more serious as well. What had started as a simple exercise began turning into structured training. Shuttle practice became regular, and physical fitness required more discipline. True to his nature, Nanna was there to guide me through this phase. He never forced strict schedules on me, yet he made sure I stayed committed to the routine we had developed. Running, stretching, and daily exercise slowly became habits that shaped my energy and health.

Thankfully, I participated in sprint events, particularly the 100-metre and 200-metre runs, and gradually started performing well at the district and state levels. Eventually, I even had the opportunity to compete at the national level. When I first stepped into those environments, it felt very different from school competitions. There were athletes from many places, each of them serious about what they were doing. I remember feeling both excited and slightly unsure of myself; that familiar "am I good enough?" feeling. But my father's guidance remained steady throughout. His approach never changed, whether the stage was small or large. He reminded me to stay calm, focus on the run, and trust the effort I had already put in.

When the event ended, and I won under his guidance, his reaction was exactly what I had come to expect from him. When I brought home those medals, there were no loud celebrations or dramatic expressions. Instead, there was the same smile I had seen many times before. That smile carried a sense of satisfaction that was difficult to describe. It was not about victory alone. It felt more like a recognition of effort, discipline, and the journey that had brought me there. And, I realised how much his encouragement had shaped every step leading to it.

Our daily life drifted back into its usual groove, balanced by the demands of school and the much-needed connection of our walks side-by-side. The conversations during those walks never stopped. Sometimes they were about serious situations he had witnessed in court. Sometimes they were simply about everyday observations. But each of those moments added something to my understanding of life.

I continue to see how seamlessly my father moved from someone who protected me as a child to someone who guided me as I began to grow up. He never made that transition obvious; it was natural and comfortable. His perspectives genuinely shaped the person I was becoming.

What remains most vivid in my memory is not any single event or achievement, but the steady presence behind them all. Whether it was a school competition, a sports practice, or a walk in the evening, he was always there with the same calm attention. And more often than not, when something went well, there would be that familiar proud smile. If you close your eyes and think of your own "steady presence," what is the one gesture they did that changed everything for you?

* * *

In other words,

In the smile that meant everything, I began to see,

How his unwavering belief strengthened me.

Not loud words, but a smile that stayed with me,

And somehow that simple moment became everything, became the world to me.

Before you turn the page:

Think of one small gesture someone in your life repeats often; a habit, a routine, or a way in which they care for you. It may be something simple that happens so regularly you hardly notice it anymore. Yet when you pause and think about it, you may realise how much comfort and reassurance it brings.

Who is that person, and what is the little gesture that stayed with you?

6

Reading the Mountain

In the high, wind-swept plateaus of the Himalayas, an old mountain guide once sat with a young traveller at the edge of a sheer cliff. Instead of pointing toward the summit, the guide spent the entire morning teaching the youth how to read the subtle shivers in the grass and the specific way a certain bird took flight before a storm. The traveller, impatient to reach the peak, asked why they weren't discussing the path ahead, but the guide smiled and said, "The mountain does not change, but the way you see the mountain will determine if you survive it." Years later, standing alone in a blinding fog on a different range, the traveller didn't look for a map; instead, he felt the grass, watched the birds, and found his way home by the instincts planted in him during those silent mornings on the cliffside.

You must be wondering why I am telling you this story. It may seem like a distant legend, far removed from the classrooms and playgrounds of my teenage years, but I ask you to read along. Wait until you reach the end of this chapter, and you will understand why these two figures matter so much. By the time we finish this part of the journey, you might even end up identifying the young traveller and the old mountain guide in your own life.

The early school years were more than just a series of morning runs and medals; they were my quiet training for life. The discipline of the damp morning tracks and the focus of the shuttle court had slowly turned into a kind of inner strength that stayed with me long after the games ended. What I once saw as just simple exercises or Nanna's stories from his law practice were, in truth, the lessons I needed to survive. He wasn't just teaching me how to win a race or a debate; he was nurturing my instincts until I could sense a change in the air long before the storm arrived. By the time I walked out of those school gates, I wasn't just carrying medals and trophies; I was carrying a compass that would show me the way.

Not long after, we went on a trip that took us through Coimbatore, Ooty, Palani, and then Madurai. By then, I had started to understand the importance of temples in a way I had not earlier. I was still more naturally drawn to landscapes; the misty hills and tall trees always reached me first, but I had begun to appreciate the beauty of temple design, the stories held in their architecture, and the history that lived in those spaces. The towering gopurams, the carved pillars, the dim inner sanctums, and the long stone corridors no longer felt like mere features of an old structure. They began to seem like vessels of memory, devotion, patience, and continuity; built not only by competent hands, but by centuries of belief. Nanna deepened that understanding. He made me see that temples are sacred spaces embodying centuries of spiritual tradition, community, and cultural identity, which helped me appreciate their deeper significance beyond physical beauty. In the ringing of bells, the tying of threads, and the sharing of prasad, he saw the diminutive acts through which people found comfort. By that age, I was beginning to see it too. I was starting to understand that a temple was not just a place people visited, but a sacrosanct space where they sought strength, serenity, reassurance, and a sense of being held by something larger than themselves.

As time went by, our discussions became even more mature. The world was opening up, and the stakes of my education were higher, yet Nanna's approach never wavered. He persisted, encouraging my involvement in sports and competitions, but the guidance he offered now was laced with practical advice and a very specific kind of calm encouragement. He never put me under strict pressure to perform or achieve. Instead, he made sure I stayed disciplined in my habits, knowing that the results would follow the effort.

This lack of external pressure allowed me to develop an internal drive. His support gave me the confidence to participate in the world without looking over my shoulder for approval. I knew that the foundation was solid. Whether I was on the shuttle court or preparing for a final exam, the discipline we had cultivated during those early morning exercises provided a sense of order. I was no longer just a daughter following her father's instructions; I was a young woman applying the principles he had modelled for me my entire life.

In our walks, I realised that my understanding of the world was a tapestry woven from his stories and my own observations. I could see the 'advocate' in the way he analysed a situation, but I saw the 'father' in the way he ensured I was equipped to handle it myself. We were two people navigating the transition of my childhood into adulthood, and the bridge between those two worlds was built on a decade of shared walks and morning runs. The safety I felt with his arm around my shoulder was now being supplemented by the safety I felt in my own judgment.

Parents often show love through their actions rather than their words, and looking back at that phase, I see his love in every shuttlecock hit and every temple history shared. He didn't need to tell me he was proud; his presence at every event and the way he spoke of my small victories to his friends told the whole story. He was grooming me for a world he knew could be difficult, but he was doing it with such a gentle hand that I only felt the strength, never the weight, of the lessons.

That realisation of dependence settles in quietly. I didn't state it then, and I didn't need to. I just knew that when I stood at the edge of any new challenge, I was looking at it through the lens he had helped me ground. The stamina I built on the track and the instincts I sharpened during our walks were the gifts he gave me, so that when I eventually had to walk without his arm on my shoulder, I would still know exactly which way to go.

The mountain guide in the high plateaus had known that the fog would eventually come, just as Nanna understood that the sheltered days of my school life would one day give way to the complex weather of adulthood. He hadn't just handed me a map of the world; he had taught me how to read the terrain for myself. By the time I reached the end of those years, the transition felt complete. I was no longer the traveller waiting for directions; I was the one who could recognise the "shivers in the grass" through the instincts we had sharpened during our walking talks. The discipline of the running track and the quiet, observed hope of the temple halls had become my internal compass. As I stood on the threshold of a larger life, I acknowledged that while the mountains of challenge ahead would never change, the way I now saw them, through the steady, reflected light of his guidance, meant I would never truly be lost.

* * *

This internal compass, built on misty tracks and ancient temple stones, was about to be tested as the horizon of my childhood finally gave way to the vast, open plains of the future. It would not be incorrect to say:

The summit was a promise, but the grass was the key,

He taught me to watch how the birds wander free.

Not a map for the road, but a light for the soul,

Reading the mountain is what sets the goal.

Before you turn the page:

Close your eyes and take a deep breath. Visualise that "safety" of a hand on your shoulder or a waist held tight. As you exhale, imagine that warmth moving from your shoulder down into your own hands. You aren't just holding a memory; you are carrying the strength they gave you. Open your eyes and take one step forward.

7

More Time, More Us

The transition from the sheltered, uniform-clad hallways of school to the sprawling, unexpected expanse of a B.Tech campus felt like a fish stepping out of a small, predictable pond and being dropped into the centre of a vast, restless ocean. The physical shift was jarring. The classrooms of my childhood, those intimate spaces where every face was familiar, were replaced by tiered lecture halls with echoing acoustics and rows of folding tablets. My teachers, who had known my name, my handwriting, and my parents' phone numbers, were gone. In their place stood professors who did not know us in the personal, everyday way our schoolteachers had, but instead spoke in the larger language of industry standards, system architecture, and global markets.

Everything was mammoth; the library felt like a maze of infinite knowledge, and the cafeteria was a sea of eclectic faces from different walks of life. It was a world of big spaces and even bigger dreams, where the air itself felt charged with the daunting, electric independence of adulthood. I distinctly remember standing in the middle of the campus courtyard during those first few weeks, watching older students rush to labs and feeling both the strangeness and excitement of a life that suddenly seemed much larger, filled with new faces, new friendships, and new possibilities. I felt small. I wondered if I was truly prepared for this sudden lack of "informals", the safety nets and constant guidance, and the heavy, sobering weight of my own choices. Was I an adult now? The question echoed in my mind every time I looked at a complex syllabus or navigated a new social circle. Perhaps that is the quiet gift of consistent love: it gives us courage to enter unfamiliar worlds without feeling entirely alone.

Yet, amidst this whirlwind of academic pressure and social evolution, my anchor remained the subdued, steady presence of my father. Our conversations evolved during this time; they were no longer just about grades or the simple mechanics of a school day, but about navigating the complexities of a life that was rapidly becoming my own.

This actualisation hit me with the force of a physical blow much later, when I first started working. I remember sitting at my laptop, overwhelmed by deadlines and uncooperative code, and finding myself snapping at my family. When they walked in to offer tea or a kind word, I would bark, "Do not disturb me!" with a frustration I couldn't contain. In those junctures of my own weakness, I saw Nanna's reflection. I understood how calmly and placidly he managed everything for decades. He never once used his fatigue as an excuse to be unkind. It was a profound lesson in maturity: I learned that keeping personal and professional life separate is very important to have a healthy relationship. It teaches children a lot as well, letting them grow in a positive environment rather than one clouded by their parents' workplace anxieties. Nanna didn't just tell me how to be a professional; he showed me that being a professional means protecting the peace of those you love.

Then, the world changed overnight. I was in my B. Tech second year, right in the thick of my core engineering subjects, when the pandemic turned our lives inward. COVID-19 was a global pandemic that spread rapidly across countries, changing everyday life with a terrifying swiftness. The virus, first reported in Wuhan, China, soon reached every corner of the world, forcing governments to impose lockdowns. Streets that were once teeming with life became eerily silent. Shops were shuttered with heavy iron locks, and we stayed inside our homes, glued to news channels that spoke constantly about rising cases, safety measures, and a thick, suffocating uncertainty about the future.

For many, it was a time of pure terror, but for us, it became a period of radical reconnection. Nanna and I spent a lot of quality time during COVID. The two to three years at home that followed was a surreal blend of global tragedy and personal sanctuary. This period made interactions more frequent. As the overall pace of life slowed to a crawl, the frantic race of "getting ahead" vanished. We inherently spent more uninterrupted time as a family than we had in years.

Our home became a microcosm of the world, and the kitchen, in particular, transformed into a laboratory of joy and experimental flavours. Nanna and I would often find ourselves in the kitchen together, trying our hand at preparing something, helping where we could, exchanging suggestions, and turning the whole process into something cheerful and alive. It was never just about cooking; it was about spending time side by side, learning, laughing, and discovering how even the simplest moments at home could become lasting memories.

I can still vividly see him wearing a kitchen towel over his shoulder, debating the yeast activation for our pizza dough. We tackled everything: pizza, samosas, pani puri, cake, and our grand Sunday project: chicken biryani. I can still smell the hot oil as we carefully drop the triangular samosas into the kadai, watching them turn that perfect golden brown. I remember the tangy, spicy aroma of the pani puri water we crafted from scratch, trying to get the tamarind and mint balance just like the street vendors he used to take me to.

"Nanna, the crust needs to be thinner," I'd argue while rolling out pizza dough.

"No, it needs to hold the weight of the cheese!" he'd reply with a wink, his eyes crinkling with a mirth I hadn't seen when office commutes bogged him down.

Those moments over the stove were where the "sharing knowledge" really happened. Between stirring pots and checking the oven, we'd talk about my interview preparations. I'd confess my fears about the job market, and he'd share stories of his own early career struggles. Our voices would compete with the sizzle of the pan and the hum of the refrigerator. When we weren't cooking, we were watching movies; everything from old classics to the latest digital releases, and playing cards on the living room floor. I can still hear the familiar, rhythmic snap of the deck being shuffled, providing a background beat to our laughter when someone tried to bluff their way through a hand.

We became a tight-knit team of four. I had my online classes and interview preparation; my brother, even while working remotely from his corner of the house, would still make time to help me navigate a few interview rounds, talking through questions with me, and offering the kind of pragmatic guidance that only an elder sibling can; Nanna was managing his responsibilities from home; and Amma, as always, was the heart of it all, taking care of us.

Though we are all busy, we made sure to sit down and talk to each other and spend quality time together. Every evening was an assembly. We would sit, watch the news and debate the current situations we saw on the screen: the politics of the lockdown, the science of the vaccine, and the changing state of the world.

Beyond the warmth of our living room, Nanna took on the role of our silent, courageous guardian. While the world felt like a dangerous place, he was the one who stepped out into the silent, ghost-town streets. Nanna used to bring every necessary item by himself, so we didn't have to go out during that period. He would come back, go through the meticulous sanitisation process, and calmly set the groceries down, never letting us feel the fear he might have been carrying.

But his empathy didn't stop at our front door. I recall watching from the window, my heart swelling with a mixture of pride and worry, as Nanna would set out to help others. I was very moved when Nanna used to buy and give daily essentials and medicines to old, aged people living nearby who couldn't leave their homes, and to his friends who were affected during COVID. He would drop bags at doorsteps, check in by phone, and provide a lifeline to people who were isolated and scared. He would return home, wash up, and never once boast about what he had done. To him, it wasn't "charity"; it was simply what a man does for his community. It shows me how humble, grounded, and helpful I should also be. He familiarised me that the measure of a person isn't what they do when everyone is watching, but what they do when the world is in shadows.

We celebrated each other's birthdays during those years with a special kind of intimacy. There were no big parties, just makeshift decorations made from old paper, homemade cakes that we had perfected in our "laboratory," and the genuine joy of being alive and together. Even as I sat at my laptop for hours, preparing for the interviews that would define my future, I apprehended that my college would not reopen until I finished my B.Tech. It's been a few years since I've been at home.

Initially, I thought I was losing my youth to the lockdown, but looking back, I discovered I was gaining something far more precious. I was getting a masterclass in character. While my B. Tech was teaching me the intricacies of engineering and logic, Nanna was teaching me the more difficult, beautiful science of being a good human. He prepared me to be a provider who doesn't quibble, a protector who doesn't boast or brag, and a person who leaves their professional burdens at the door to make room for love. Those years at home weren't a hiatus in my life; they were the foundation of the invincible woman I was becoming.

* * *

When life unexpectedly slows, we begin to notice how the simplest days shape the deepest parts of who we become. And thus,

With more time and more us, the rushing world grew slow,

And ordinary days had deeper truths to show.

In laughter, care, and thoughts that gently stirred,

I discovered how love lives in what goes unsaid, unheard.

Before you turn the page:

Send a simple message right now to one person, perhaps a parent, friend, neighbour, or elder, saying: "Just checking in, how are you today?"

You'll receive a warm reply almost instantly, reminding you how even a small gesture can brighten someone's day and solidify a relationship.

8

Grammar of Care

In our house, love was never a loud or decorative thing; it was a series of modest, rhythmic adjustments to the day's climate. It was the sound of a bedsheet being pulled into the wash before shame could settle, the patient cooling of a dinner plate while a meeting ran late, and the weight of a blanket appearing over my shoulders when sleep finally claimed the workday. Nanna didn't believe in the performance of kindness; he believed in its utility. He moved through the house with a silent, steady discipline, absorbing the friction of the world so that I didn't have to. This was the era where "normal" became a sanctuary, and I discovered that the deepest form of respect lies not in words, but in the absence of hesitation when someone meets you in your most vulnerable moments.

By then, the pandemic had stopped feeling like a passing storm and had become the weather of our days. Life had slowed, and we saw more of one another than we usually did. There was more overlap between our routines, more chances to witness each other in ordinary, unguarded moments. My bond with Nanna deepened through repeated closeness and the long stretch of shared days. That phase taught me that intimacy in a family is rarely built in grand scenes. More often, it is formed in the repetition of ordinary living.

Even in that difficult period, Nanna's instinct was always to look beyond himself. His sense of responsibility did not end at our gate. From time to time, I became aware of the understated ways he extended help to families who were struggling, especially when children were involved. He would step in where he could, arrange what was needed, and then move on without ever making it something to be spoken about at length. That was his way. Some forms of kindness leave the deepest mark precisely because they arrive without spectacle. They do not seek witness, gratitude, or remembrance; they simply meet the moment and move on. Perhaps that is why such acts stay with us. They remind us that goodness is often most real when it is least advertised. Nanna never turned kindness into performance. To him, if someone needed help and he could offer it, the matter was simple. His care was practical, unadorned, and sincere, reflecting a true unselfishness that we can all aspire to.

That same quality revealed itself even more powerfully inside the home. One morning, I woke up with the familiar heaviness of my menstrual cycle, that dull ache low in the body. There were distress and a drag in my limbs. Then, in a second, that ordinary discomfort turned into embarrassment. I saw the bedsheet and admitted I had bled through in the night. The stain stood out against the fabric, impossible to miss. For a moment, my body felt like something I wanted to hide from everyone, even though it was my own. It was the old reflex many girls grow up with; the urge to cover, conceal, clean, make it disappear before anyone notices.

I got up quickly, still slightly embarrassed. Amma saw it. Nanna did too. I stepped away for a moment, still flustered, and when I came back, the bedsheet had already been removed. Nanna had taken it aside for washing. There was no expression of affliction on his face, no forced casualness, no sentence meant to manage the situation. He did not stare, and he did not avert his eyes either. He treated it exactly the way he would have treated any accidental spill in the house. Not because he did something dramatic, but because he made it so downright normal.

In our home, periods were never treated as shameful or secret. If I needed pads, he brought them without hesitation. There was no embarrassment in his manner, no sense that this belonged only to Amma and not to him. During those days, Nanna was usually more attentive in small ways. He noticed when I was uncomfortable. He made sure I had what I needed. He was patient with my moods without naming them and without making me feel guilty for them. He never publicised acceptance. He just practised it.

What stayed with me most was the dignity of that normalcy. There is often some version of shame, awkwardness, or concealment attached to menstruation, even when nobody says it directly. But Nanna never allowed that atmosphere to grow around me. He never made me feel that my body was inconvenient or something to be handled behind closed doors with embarrassment. It was simpler than that. It was normal. And because it was normal, it was powerful. Respect in our home was not considered as a principle. It appeared in behaviour; in the scarcity of disgust, in the lack of hesitation, and in the way he protected my comfort. That morning passed, the sheet was washed, and the day moved on. But something in me remained steadier because of it. So often, what stays with us is not what people say about love or respect, but the quiet ways they make our most vulnerable moments feel less frightening and more human.

Then another shift came. My brother moved to Canada, and the house changed shape. Until then, our family rhythm had always moved around four people. Suddenly, it was the three of us: Amma, Nanna, and me. The difference was deeply felt. Homes absorb departures in subtle ways. A chair remains empty more often. Certain conversations disappear. The house became more concentrated, more intimate in its own way. We adjusted to that new geometry gradually. What one absence left behind was filled, in some unseen way, by greater attentiveness among the three of us.

By then, I had started working from home. That brought with it a different kind of tiredness; less physical perhaps, but constant and draining in its own way. Timelines blurred. One task rolled into the next. Work did not always end when official hours ended; it lingered in tabs left open, unfinished responses, and the restlessness that follows you even after you stand up from the chair. There were evenings when that tiredness would settle over me before I had fully admitted it. I would leave things half-done, the laptop still open, the day trailing behind me in unfinished tabs and replies. And yet, even then, care had a way of reaching me. A blanket would be placed over me, and the tiredness of the day would feel a little lighter. Moments like these made me look at Nanna differently. They showed me that even while carrying the weight of his own days, he remained attentive to ours.

He would return from court carrying responsibilities and pressures of his own, but he never allowed professional strain to harden the atmosphere at home. He did not make his work everyone else's burden. He balanced work and family so naturally that, as a child, I had almost mistaken it for ease. It was maturity and restraint. Only later did I understand the discipline hidden inside that calm, the skill of keeping life's dust and din from settling on the people you love. It taught me that care does not always arrive in dramatic gestures; sometimes it lives in the steady effort to make sure home continues to feel like shelter. In that sense, even the smallest acts carried meaning: they said, without words, that someone had noticed your tiredness and wanted to make the day gentler before it ended.

Our evenings gradually began to organise themselves around my schedule. If my meetings ran late, dinner ran late too. Even if the food were ready earlier, Nanna would often wait so we could eat together. He would call from court or while returning home and ask whether my meetings were over and whether we should wait for dinner. There was no complaint in it, no hint that my work had disrupted the household. Instead, what I felt from him was accommodation. My new life, with all its long hours and odd timings, was not treated like an inconvenience. Room was made for it. To be waited for at the table is no small thing.

He also had the habit of calling on the way back to ask if we needed anything from outside. But what touched me most were the calls shaped by memory. He would say he was passing by a particular place and ask whether I wanted something I liked from there. A puff, a cake, a familiar snack, something he knew I enjoyed. They told me that even in the middle of his own workday, he was still thinking of us with detail. Love often hides in these crumbs and clues, in those who remember the little things and return carrying them home.

Nanna had a way of making life feel more settled. He noticed things early, often before anyone else had even thought about them, and took care of them so naturally that it did not draw attention to itself. He planned, remembered small details, and paid attention to what each of us needed, with a steadiness that shaped the atmosphere of the house. There are some people whose care is woven so fully into everyday life that you only realise much later how much they were holding together. He believed in discipline, but never in a way that felt harsh; with him, it came with encouragement and the expectation that we were capable of more. He was happy with our progress, whether it was something big or something that might have seemed small to others, and that kind of belief has a way of staying with a person. Perhaps that is one of the quintessential gifts a parent can give: not just support, but the sense that you are seen, trusted, and gently guided at the same time. Even when he said little, his presence was reassuring. He could sense worry, hesitation, or tiredness without needing everything to be explained, and responded in ways that made things feel more manageable. He brought order into life, but also warmth, and that combination made home feel not just provided for, but deeply cared for.

One incident from around that time remains especially clear in my mind. I wanted to go to another city to meet my friends. There was unsettling news in circulation about girls going missing, and the atmosphere felt even more tense because of a political rally connected to the elections. Nanna was uneasy about my going, and he had every reason to be. But what I remember is the balance with which he responded. He did not dismiss my wish, and he did not impose a blunt refusal either. He found a way to hold both concern and trust together. He came with me, dropped me there safely, and later picked me up himself. Later, I understood its depth. He was not trying to control my movement. He was trying to absorb the risk himself, so I did not have to face it alone. That was his way again and again: not to cage me, but to cover me.

Now, what stands out is not one dramatic event, but a pattern. Those years revealed the fine grain of his love. They showed me how care can be understated, how dignity can be normalised, how protection can exist without possession, and how responsibility can be carried without announcement. He helped those in need without spectacle. He handled my most private discomfort without awkwardness. He waited for me at the dinner table. He remembered the food I liked. He closed my laptop when sleep overtook me. He returned from court without bringing the hardness of work into the house. He made room for my life even while living his own fully. That was his gift. He never made acceptance into a speech, or love into a display. He turned both into a habit. And because of that, they became the very definition of what felt normal to me.

In my understanding of love, I can say:

Through the grammar of care, he translated the heavy and the loud

Into a tender silence that lifted the shame and the cloud.

Is true devotion found in the grand scene, or in a blanket's fold,

In the strength of a hand that protects without trying to hold?

Before you turn the page:

Make a list of three small things a loved one has done for you without being asked. Then ask yourself: were those small things, or were they the structure of safety in my life?

9

Between Journeys and Goodbyes

In the sacred geometry of Lord Krishna and Goddess Radharani's relationship and devotion, life is not viewed as a straight line, but as a divine dance between the soul and its purpose. It teaches us that true relationship is not found in possession, but in the grace of presence; a delicate balance between holding on with devoutness and letting go with faith. When we face the sudden landslides of uncertainty and the uphill treks of life's challenges, we learn that strength is not the absence of struggle, but the ability to remain grounded in our values while the world shifts around us. Their story reminds us that even when the physical path becomes unclear, a heart anchored in selfless love and steady duty can transform any moment of reserved meditation or sudden storm into a step toward a more profound, more fundamental truth.

This philosophy became the very base upon which I have written this episode of my life. It is the lens through which I began to see the ordinary moments of 2023; the dinners, the drives, and the subdued evenings; as something far more profound. As you read this chapter, you will come to know the specific ways a father's silent protection acts as an anchor in a restless world. I am so eager to share with you how a simple television routine turned into a masterclass in perspective, how a family found its fullness in the mountains of the North and the forests of the East, and how I finally learned that love is most visible in the things we remember for one another. You will see how, even when the world feels like it is stretching thin, the bonds we nurture in the speechless hours are what truly keep us whole.

Our home had changed by then, and we were still learning the shape of that change. With my brother in Canada, it was just Amma, Nanna, and me at home, and that smaller circle created its own rhythm. I was working from home, which meant the boundaries between professional time and family time had softened. The day did not end with a commute or a doorway. It dissolved gradually, and in that gradualness, a new routine entered our lives. After both of us finished work, Nanna and I began watching *Radha Krishna* and *the Mahabharat* together. At first, it was just something we did in the evening, a shared habit to settle into after the day's responsibilities. But slowly, it became far more than that. Those serials opened a space between us where conversation, culture, and perspective began to grow in an easy, unforced way.

Watching them together was not passive. I was not merely sitting beside him while mythological stories played on screen. I was beginning to enter them through his eyes. In *the Mahabharatam*, every conflict seemed to carry layers: dharma against attachment, loyalty against truth, love against pride, justice against destiny. In *Radhu Krishna*, relationships were not shown as simple emotions but as piety, surrender, value, and balance. What made

those evenings so memorable was not just the serials themselves, but what followed them. Once an episode ended, Nanna and I would sometimes drift into casual post-episode discussions. They were never formal, never heavy, never like a lecture delivered by a father who wanted to instruct his daughter. They arose inevitably as we remained seated, talking about an important scene, a misunderstanding between characters, a moment of sacrifice, or a conflict shaped by ego. Sometimes we spoke about relationships, on other days about values. Sometimes, he underscored the different ways people understand duty, affection, or pain. He had a way of making these conversations feel light in tone and deep in effect.

What once felt ordinary now feels surreal. Thus, I can say that those discussions changed my perspective. They did not do so all at once, nor did they do so loudly. But they altered the angle from which I began to see situations and people. Through those episodes and the thoughts that followed, I began to understand that life is rarely as direct as it appears in the moment. Every action has a context. Every person carries a reason. Every relationship has unseen layers. Nanna's reflections made those stories feel less like distant cultural inheritance and more like living guides to human nature. He made them eye-opening for me. He showed me how values are not abstract things placed on a pedestal; they are tested in ordinary life, in difficult choices, in moments of anger, confusion, responsibility, and restraint. In that phase, I gained knowledge, yes, but more than that, I gained a more grounded way of seeing.

That same period was also defined by another routine that revealed his care in an entirely different register. After I started working, especially when my work hours became longer, dinner at home began to depend on my schedule. Meetings ran late, tasks stretched out, and evenings often lost their natural stopping point.

Many nights, I finished work later than expected, but he still preferred to sit and have dinner together rather than eat first and move on. There was something tremendously comforting in that. It told me, without ever saying so, that my place at the table mattered. Even now, when I think of it, I find myself wondering who else would care that consistently; calling every day, checking in, and holding that space open until I arrived.

There was another form of tenderness I remember clearly. I would often ask Nanna for a head massage, and he would always do it for me with such patience and care. There was something genuinely reassuring in that simple gesture. He never made it seem like a burden or a favour; he did it with the ease of someone for whom caring was second nature. What might seem like a small thing from the outside often becomes, in memory, one of the most lasting expressions of love. It is in these ordinary acts of comfort that affection settles with unusual intensity into the heart.

Life moved as usual and then came the North India trip, one of the most memorable vacations we took together. It was long, varied, and full of wonder. We started from Agra, then went to Vrindavan, Mathura, Dehradun, Chandigarh, Manali, Amritsar, and Delhi, before returning to our hometown. For Amma and me, it was our first time visiting North India, and that alone gave the trip a special charge. Everything felt new. The places, the people, the food, the dressing styles, the conversations, the landscapes; each place had its own personality, and each stop widened something inside me. Nanna was very happy throughout because he was able to show us so many places. I could sense that happiness clearly. There is a particular joy in taking the people you love somewhere they have never been before and watching the world unfold before them.

One of the brightest memories from that trip was our first snow experience. I had seen snow in photographs and films, but encountering it in actual life was something else entirely. It made all of us lighter. I could see Nanna and Amma becoming like children in front of it, playing, enjoying, reacting with a kind of open delight that made me want to preserve every second. Throughout the trip, I served as Nanna and Amma's personal photographer. I was always capturing them; standing together, laughing, exploring, looking at something with wonder. Taking those photographs did not feel like a task. It felt like a privilege. Through the camera, I was also seeing them afresh: not only as parents, but as two people with curiosity, playfulness, and joy.

And yet, the trip also carried a reminder of how watchful he always was. One leg of the trip took us from Chandigarh to Manali by bus. It was an ordinary bus, booked then and there, not some especially planned or luxurious arrangement. What made us uneasy was that a landslide had occurred the day before. Amma and I were understandably sceptical and concerned. But Nanna trusted his instinct that we would reach without any problem. What he did next has stayed with me with particular clarity: he remained awake the whole night. Not intermittently awake. The whole night. He stayed up because Amma and I should feel safe. I even told him that he could sleep in between while I was awake, but he did not. He watched over the journey from beginning to end. That image remains crystalline to me: a moving bus, a dark road, a mountainous uncertainty outside, and him holding himself alert simply because his first instinct was to protect. He did not say much about it. He just did it. Perhaps that is how the most significant care often appears—not in grand words, but in the silent decisions that let someone else sleep without fear.

That trip taught Amma and me a significantly beyond geography. We learned about culture, food, people, dressing styles, and the many small differences that make each place feel distinct. Travel with him was never just movement through places. It was education through experience. It was attention sharpened by his presence. Even the way he pointed things out, never making it feel like a lecture, always making it feel like a discovery, left a mark on me. I could see, more and more, how much of his way of seeing the world was slowly becoming part of mine.

Later that year, the house filled out again in a completely different way. My brother's visit from Canada had originally been planned for December, but he preponed it and came earlier. He wanted to come quickly, even though tensions between Canada and India were high at the time. When he arrived, the feeling in the house changed immediately. We were four again. That alone carried warmth. I could feel the family bond strongly during that period, not because anyone spoke about it, but because we slipped back into a fuller rhythm so organically. We went to the stadium. Nanna introduced my brother to many of his friends, and the two of them went out together. He also brought many of my brother's favourite food items, and Amma cooked a lot because he was home. There was affection in every direction.

That phase was also full of simple pleasures. We watched movies together. Two films were released during that month, and we went for both. We had pizza while watching movies and went out for ice cream. We cooked together at home. None of these details is grand on paper, but they hold the texture of family life. They are the kinds of memories that feel ordinary while you are living them and become more pronounced only later. That month had that fullness: food, outings, film plans, shared time, easy happiness. It felt like a house breathing at its reflexive and intuitive capacity again.

During that visit, we suddenly decided to take a trip with family friends to Maredumilli. That incident had a completely different energy from the North India trip. It felt rawer, more rooted in forest, terrain, and local life. We saw tribal villages and got a glimpse of how people there lived and what food they ate. We took a car to reach Gudisa, a viewpoint, and the drive itself felt extraordinary because we were travelling through the forest with no internet. There is a very particular feeling that comes when phones stop being useful, and you have to rely on people and place. We had no signal, and on the way to the waterfall, we kept asking the few people we saw on the roads for directions. Most of them were from the tribal communities there. The world suddenly felt less controlled and more alive.

The waterfall trek remains one of the most vivid parts of that trip. Very few people were there, and the place had an untouched, peaceful quality that made the effort worthwhile the moment we arrived. But reaching it took work. We had to trek, and parts of the path were so steep that I worried we might slip. Then, at one point, we watched a tribal woman carrying her child and walking with ease across the same terrain that had made us cautious, without slippers. That sight shifted something in me. It reminded me how relative difficulty can be, how quickly comfort makes us forget the capacities people build when life demands it.

Near that waterfall, Nanna and I meditated together. That memory remains as the unvarnished fact in my mind. The setting itself was enough to quiet the mind; the water, the rock, the sense of being far away from ordinary noise. To sit there beside him in meditation felt like entering another layer of the trip, one that was not about movement but about stillness. We also climbed the mountain there, and by the time we returned to the main town, the day had already become unforgettable. Then came another sensory memory: we had the famous bamboo chicken. It felt like the perfect end to a day that had already carried forest, effort, silence, perspective, and shared presence.

One scene from that trip has stayed with me almost symbolically. A cow came near Nanna in a way that did not feel accidental. It came as if it had known him for a long time and began cuddling against him with an ease that startled us. People often say that positive people attract animals, and in that moment, I could see exactly what they meant. The affection seemed instinctive. It felt as though the animal had recognised something in him that needed no introduction. Some moments resist analysis and remain simply as signs.

Then, after all that fullness, came departure again. A week later, my brother had to leave, and we all went to Hyderabad to give him a send-off. That farewell remains intimately etched in me because, for the first time, I saw Nanna's eyes tear up as my brother was leaving. It was not a dramatic display, just a visible softening, a brief breaking of composure. But it said everything. I had seen his love in protection, in care, in memory, in discipline, in presence. In that moment, I saw it in grief too; in the ache of parting, in the helplessness that comes even to strong people when someone they love must go away again.

As I sat by the window to write this chapter of my life, I felt age altering the lens through which I see the world, and I finally began to understand how much of Nanna's inner world he had been passing on to me all along; lessons, sensibilities, and tastes that I have come to value with immense tenderness over the years. A father and daughter often understand each other like sunlight and a window; one entering softly, the other slowly learning how to hold and reflect that light. He always insisted that the songs and films of his era carried a certain soul, and lately I have begun to feel that for myself. On a hot summer evening, as a gentle breeze shakes the curtains and moves through my hair, I sit with a cup of tea and find a rooted, resonant, unspoken peace in those old melodies. He also taught me to widen my vision while travelling; where I once looked only for natural landscapes, he taught me to notice architecture, atmosphere, and the greatness held within old places. Now, my own travels begin with a different kind of attentiveness. From listening to his stories about our ancestors and sharing those evenings of conversation and reflection beside him, I began to understand what values look like in lived life and how essential it is to remain grounded. People say everything happens for a reason, and though I may not always understand the reasons behind life's arrangements, I know this much: I want to live in a way that makes him proud, and to help carry forward the love, strength, and dreams he poured into our family.

As I finish my half cold cup of tea, and feel my eyes well up, I have to admit that,

In between journeys and goodbyes, what was it I came to see;

That every road he chose with love was moulding me?

Why do farewells leave behind the truths we failed to name,

And why does the heart read nearness best when life no longer stays the same?

Before you turn the page:

Request your favorite old song on the radio or play it at home, then hum, sway, or even twirl along with it. Pay attention to how a simple melody can lift your mood and, in the most innocent way, return you to the memory of someone whose love still lingers in your heart.

10

Silences Split My Life

That morning began like so many Indian mornings do: under the soft authority of ritual, routine, and small domestic movement. It was the day of Nagulachaviti, a day associated with reverence, prayer, and a certain inherited tenderness toward faith. On that day, many women visited temples, especially those associated with serpent deities, offering milk, turmeric, flowers, and prayers for protection, family well-being, and peace.

There is something distinctly rooted about such days. They carry not just devotion, but continuity. They connect the present household to older rhythms of belief, to mothers and grandmothers and their mothers before them. The sunrise harboured that atmosphere. It felt sacred in the ordinary way sacredness often enters Indian life, not through thunder but preparation.

Amma was planning to drop Ammama (maternal grandmother) back at her home. On the way, they wanted to stop at the temple in Nagulapadu, a place known in the region and spoken of with a certain reverence. I had wanted to visit it for a long time. Temples like that do not stand in memory merely as buildings. They gather a presence around themselves. Nagulapadu was one of those places; old enough to feel storied, beloved enough to feel alive in public faith. I imagined the familiar temple textures even before we got there: the worn stone under bare feet, the mingled fragrance of camphor, jasmine, turmeric, incense, and dust; the rustle of sarees; the metallic echo of bells; the brief seriousness that settles over people as they fold their hands before entering. I wanted to be part of that day, part of that stream of worshippers moving toward something ancient and reassuring.

Nanna and I had another routine too. We had the habit of going to the stadium daily. It had become part of the scaffolding of our life; so familiar that it seemed unremarkable, and because it seemed unremarkable, it also seemed permanent. That is the danger of love lived through routine: you do not fathom, while you are inside it, how much faith you place in repetition. You believe the next morning will come arranged in the same way, with the same voices, the same habits, the same people stepping in and out of rooms. That morning, when I asked Nanna whether I should go with Amma and Ammama or come with him instead, he said I could go to the temple if I wanted. He had work in court and could not join us. Nothing in his tone carried warning. Nothing asked to be remembered more carefully than usual.

And yet the morning is carved into me now with painful precision.

Since Ammama was going back home, Nanna stepped into the practical tenderness that came so naturally to him. He went to buy vegetables and a few essentials she might need. I can still imagine that market scene as though I were standing at its edge, watching him move through it. The market would have been alive in the way Indian vegetable markets always are: green heaps of coriander damp with morning water, stacks of brinjals catching purple light, tomatoes glowing red in cane baskets, the smell of curry leaves and mud, the calls of vendors announcing freshness with practised insistence, the passing friction of cloth bags, bicycles, and bargaining voices. Such places are full of life in a very grounded way. Nothing theatrical. Just the abundance of daily needs. And there he was in the middle of it, buying fresh vegetables, choosing what Ammama might require, thinking one step ahead as he always did. He was never careless about care. Even affection, with him, had an administrative intelligence. He did not merely feel for people; he prepared for them.

Before we left, he also told Amma to carry a water bottle, just in case I needed it during the trip. That detail undoes me even now. Out of all the things a mind could hold on to from that morning, it returns to that water bottle. That he was still thinking of my thirst before I had even begun the journey. That in the most ordinary corner of the day, he was already making provisions for my comfort. Love often survives most vividly in these domestic footnotes. Not in speeches, not in dramatic declarations, but in instructions like carry water, take this, eat before you go, call me when you reach.

Just before I was about to get ready, he asked me if I would come to the stadium.

That was the last thing he said to me.

At the time, it was just another sentence. Familiar. Casual. Folded seamlessly into the morning. I did not pause over it. I did not know it would become one of those ordinary lines that later grows unbearably luminous in memory. Then Amma, Ammama, and I left for the temple, and he went to the stadium.

The day did not fracture all at once. It began with inconvenience, not catastrophe. The bus came late, very late, and we had to wait for nearly an hour and a half. I remember the irritation of that delay, the kind that feels so trivial in the moment and so impossible to recover later. We were ready, dressed, mentally set for the temple, and yet forced to stand there waiting, held up by something as impersonal as public transport. By the time the bus finally came, and we got on, we had only just crossed our city when my phone rang.

It was the gym trainer, someone close to our family and personally known to us.

Her words did not fully register at first. They arrived as fragments.

Nanna had fallen.

He had been admitted to the hospital.

There are moments when language reaches you before validity does. The sentence lands, but the mind refuses to build its implications. For a few seconds, maybe longer, I lived in that refusal. Fallen? What did that mean? Fainted? Slipped? Injury? Something minor? Something temporary? Surely something temporary. We got off the bus immediately and took an auto back. From that point onward, time lost all ordinary proportion. The road became too long. Traffic became offensive. Every second felt misplaced. And inside me, something had begun to unravel.

On the way to the hospital, there was no god I did not pray to. No name I did not invoke. My thoughts were not coherent enough to be called thoughts. They were flashes, pleas, bargains, desperate bits of faith thrown upward in all directions. Let him be okay. Let this be small. Let us reach in time. Let him sit up when he sees us. Let someone say we panicked for nothing. Let the doctor smile and call it exhaustion. Let this day go back to being ordinary.

That is what the mind does when fear becomes too large. It starts trying to rewrite reality before it has fully arrived.

By the time we reached the hospital, many of his friends were already there. I remember seeing their faces before I remember anything else. Familiar faces, but not arranged familiarly. Too still. Too gathered. Too grave. Amma, Ammama, and I kept asking what had happened, whether he was fine, whether someone had seen him, and whether a doctor was attending to him. But the answers came strangely. Some people said he was fine. Some said nothing at all. Some avoided our eyes. Some looked at us with a helplessness that frightened me more than any clear sentence could have. Silence had already begun to say what nobody wanted to pronounce.

Then they took only me inside.

I walked in carrying hope so stubborn it was almost irrational. He was lying on the bed. No doctor was around. That itself was wrong, but even then, my mind refused to assemble the truth. I moved toward him. I tried to wake him. I touched his hand.

It was cold.

I can still feel that moment as something physical inside me. The coldness did not just belong to his skin. It entered me. It split the room. It made the world unfamiliar in a single instant.

And still, still, I was not ready to understand. My brain stopped behaving like a thinking organ and became something else entirely, something stunned, suspended, half-shattered. He had been healthy that morning. He had been buying vegetables. He had told Amma to take a water bottle. He had asked me to come to the stadium. How could a body move from that life into this stillness in a matter of hours? I remember trying to wake him again. I remember asking where the doctor was. I remember asking his friends what had happened. I remember feeling as though I was speaking from underwater.

What I received in return was silence.

Not the ordinary silence of a room with no noise. A denser silence. The kind that gathers when truth is already present, and language has failed before it. Then Amma and Ammama came in. And in that silence, the meaning finally reached us. Not like a sentence. Like an impact. Like the sky had dropped.

Without warning, his heart gave way, and with it, the world I knew changed forever. Nanna was gone.

Even writing those words does not match the force of that fruition. It was not sorrow first. It was a rupture. It was disbelief so total that my mind stopped comprehending life and death in any normal way. Everything in me went numb and feverish at once. I was crying, but the crying felt far away, as though it belonged to someone else and was happening through me. My mind had begun flashing scenes at the speed and in the disobedience of memory unchained. Childhood mornings. Temple outings. Birthday cakes. His voice calling out to me. His hand resting on my head. The stadium. Bike rides. Food. Songs. Advice. Protection. Irritation. Routine. Affection. It all came at me in fragments, as if my whole life with him had turned into a broken film reel and every frame wanted to be seen before I lost the right to see him breathe again.

I remember an almost animal thought taking hold of me: this cannot be the end of a person who was alive this morning.

Grief had not yet organised itself into grief. It was shock, refusal, collapse, noise inside the skull, and a strange frozen vacancy all at once. And for a long moment, nothing moved forward. The mind stood there, staring at the fact of it, unable to gather the scattered pieces into anything that resembled meaning. In that first stunned stillness, there was only the impossible truth sitting heavily in the room: that a person who had been alive that morning had, somehow, already become part of the past. Nothing in me knew how to cross that distance. The body remained where it was, but the mind could not move beyond that single fact. It kept circling it, returning to it, refusing and recognising it in the same breath. That is what the earliest moments of loss are like for anyone who has loved deeply: not sorrow in its full shape yet, but a stunned suspension in which reality arrives faster than the heart can bear it.

After the procedures, we brought him home. We donated his eyes. That decision felt unbearably fitting. Even in death, he would continue to give. But no action that day felt fully unpretentious. The phone rang incessantly as people struggled to reconcile the news with the reality of a life lived so intentionally; it seemed impossible that someone so mindful of his health, so disciplined in his habits, and so meticulous about his choices could be taken so suddenly. We live in an era in which we read, learn, and labour to master the art of well-being, alongside a world of people becoming increasingly conscious of how they move and what they consume. We treat wellness as a shield, yet life remains stubbornly unpredictable, eventually reaching a point where all human effort meets its natural limit. In that moment, we are forced to bow before a will more potent, more emphatic than our own, acknowledging that when it is time for a soul to depart, no amount of discipline can delay or turn back the tide. Life and death move in a cycle far beyond our reach, leaving us with the painful, humbling task of accepting what no love, no strength, and no preparation could ever prevent.

To be honest, I was not in a state to answer anyone. I cried. I informed my brother. Relatives began to arrive. Friends came. Then more people came. And more. The house could not contain the scale of feeling that followed him.

The road was filled with people.

That is not an exaggeration. The entire road was packed with those who had come to see him one last time. I heard people praising him, recalling him, grieving him, speaking of what he had done for them, how he had helped them, what he had meant in their lives. Standing in the middle of that human tide, I understood something devastating and beautiful at once: I had known him as my father, but he had belonged in significant ways to so many others, too. His life had travelled far beyond the rooms of our home. His goodness had entered other households, other struggles, other memories. The road itself seemed to testify to it.

After Nanna's passing, a daughter like me discovers that the world has not just changed, but has fundamentally reconfigured itself into something unrecognisable. To the outsider, life and death are merely the predictable swing of a pendulum; a natural cycle as certain as the tide, and they might wonder why we fret over the inevitable. But they do not understand that for a daughter, a father isn't just a person; he is the very gravity that holds her world in place. When that gravity vanishes, the void it creates is not a hollow space that time can fill, but a permanent shift in the atmosphere. Life will never be the same because the silent permission to be a child has been revoked; the "back" I always felt behind me is now a vast, open expanse of wind.

As we were bringing Nanna back home after the eye donation, the world outside continued to move with a cruel, indifferent rhythm. Through the window of the vehicle, I saw a little girl on the sidewalk, barely a toddler, trying to take her first clumsy steps. Her father was bent over her, his large hands methodically encircling her tiny ones, bracing her against the air, helping her find a balance she hadn't yet mastered. Watching them, I felt a sob catch in my throat that I couldn't suppress. I broke down completely because, in that simple, everyday sight, I saw the magnitude of my loss. I conceded then that my anchor had been cut loose. My father was gone, never to return, but like that little child, a part of me remains suspended in that same state of waiting.

I find myself drowning in a million questions; some logical, some illogical, and many that feel purely desperate. I want to scream at the sky and ask God, "Why?" Why my father? What did I do wrong to deserve this silence? What mistake did he make to be taken away while he was so full of life? Was it too early for him, or was it somehow too late for the dreams we still had to build? I don't know which book to read or which path to take to find these answers. I wonder if even God, with all His power, could answer me in a way that makes sense, or if any answer matters if it doesn't bring my Nanna back to me. Is it truly necessary for death to come? Does it have to be this final, this cold, this absolute?

A hidden corner of my heart still waits at the door, listening for the familiar sound of his arrival. I find myself expecting him to walk in with the heavy bags of vegetables, having picked out my favourites with that silent, meticulous supervision of his. I wait to show him the new dresses I love to wear, or to share my successes and failures, looking for the grounding look in his eyes that tells me everything will be okay. There is a deep, quiet ache in the actuality that I can no longer ask him for the one thing I need most. I want to reach out through the silence and request him just one last time: "Nanna, come along and walk with me." But the door remains still, and I am left to navigate a world of "why" without the only person who ever had all the answers.

In the weeks after, time lost its edges. December arrived, but I did not feel as though I had moved into another month so much as drifted into another version of certitude. We began going through some of his things, the way families do when anguish forces practical work upon them. In his suitcase, among papers and old belongings, we found a drawing. Amma looked at it and said it was mine; my first drawing, the one I had made when I was barely 3 years old. There were also a few progress reports, including my brother's report cards with his grades. I cannot fully explain what that discovery did to me. Surprise, happiness, numbness, ache; everything rose together. He had kept that drawing safe for twenty years. A small piece of paper from my childhood had travelled with him into adulthood, work, movement, responsibility, and all the seasons in between. He had preserved our growing years in secret, like a private museum of love.

That was when the depth of his affection struck me in a new way. Not because I had doubted it before, but because love seen in preserved objects becomes almost unbearable. He had kept evidence of us. Our efforts. Our grades. Our little attempts at expression. Every memory of ours had mattered to him. Every milestone. Every trace. And I recognised then how much I had meant to him, and how impossible it now felt that I could not return that understanding to him in the same language of living presence.

So many things began changing after that. Temples, for one. Earlier, when he planned trips, I had wanted only nature: hills, forests, open skies, waterfalls. He would tell me to notice temples too: their history, architecture, atmosphere, the peace they offer, the grandeur held inside old stone. I did not understand him fully then. Now I do. Now I find myself planning temple visits first. Now I sit before an idol and understand how human beings cling to hope in the tiniest gestures: bells, threads, prasad, folded hands. Little acts, big faith. After him, I began finding authentic peace in temples.

The same happened with old songs. He used to say the songs and films from his time had a depth of their own. I hear that now. I hear it properly. Their melodies have become places where my suffering can sit without being disturbed. What once seemed old-fashioned now feels deeply alive. In their slowness, their ache, their tenderness, I find him again.

And life, without asking whether I was ready, moved me from dependence into responsibility. From going to temples with him to going alone. From planning trips together to planning them on my own. From being a passenger princess to driving. From assuming he would always handle the unseen details to learning to manage every little thing on my own. There is pain in that transformation, but also a strange strength. Somewhere inside it, I can feel myself becoming the woman he had always hoped I would be.

I may never understand why life can be so generous one moment and so merciless the next. Some losses do not arrive as lessons; they arrive as absences too vast to explain. But if distress has taught me anything, it is that love does not end where a life does. It changes form. It becomes memory, discipline, faith, responsibility, and the quiet strength to continue. And so, in the life I build from here, I want to honour him by holding close all that he placed within us: his values, his courage, his care, and his unshaken belief in family.

At this point, with trembling hands, all I can write is.

Silence split my life in ways no language could repair,

One morning stood complete, and then he was not there.

How does a daughter cross the world when all she knew falls still?

By carrying his love within her pulse, her prayer, her will.

Before you turn the page:

Pause for a moment and think of one quiet act of care that once held your life together. Not a lavish sacrifice, just something small and steady: a meal kept aside for you, a light left on, a question asked at the right time, a presence that made your day feel less heavy. Sit with that remembrance for a minute. Then ask yourself whether you ever truly recognised the love inside that ordinary gesture. We often understand too late that what looked small was never small at all. It was someone making room for us inside the burdens of their own life. And if your heart allows it, softly say, ***"I love you,"*** *to the person who still lives in that memory.*

Closing Reflection: If Nanna Were Here

If Nanna were alive, I would crawl back through the clock. I would tear the pages out of the calendar until I found myself standing in the hallway of a normal, boring afternoon. I wouldn't knock. I wouldn't wait. I would just walk in and find him exactly where he used to be, sitting in that chair, the one that holds the shape of his shoulders better than any person ever could.

I would watch him for a long time before he noticed me. I'd watch the way he adjusted his glasses, the way he squinted at the news, and the way he'd let out that specific, tired sigh; the one that wasn't a complaint, but just the sound of a man who had carried a family on his back for forty years and was finally letting the air out.

And then, he would see me.

He'd say that thing he always said; that phrase that used to feel like a chore to answer, but now feels like the only music I want to hear. He'd ask, *"Have you eaten?"* or *"Are you alright?"* or he'd just call my name in that voice that sounded like home.

I would fall to my knees at his feet. I wouldn't care if it looked dramatic. I wouldn't care about being an "adult" or being "composed." I would bury my face in his lap, and I would weep into the fabric of his trousers until it was soaked. I would tell him, *"Nanna, the world is so much louder without you. It's so much colder. There is no one left to check the locks* *at night. There is no one left whose pride in me doesn't have a price tag."*

I would look at his hands; those beautiful, weathered, honest hands. I'd memorise every vein, every liver spot, every callus earned from a life of "doing without" so that I could "have." I'd press them to my cheeks, and I wouldn't let go. I'd tell him I'm sorry for every time I checked my phone while he was talking. I'm sorry for every time I rolled my eyes at his advice. I'm sorry for the times I thought I was smarter than him just because I knew how to use a computer, when he was the one who knew how to survive a storm.

I'd ask him to tell me the story again. The one about the struggle. The one he narrated as a bedtime story. The one about the day I was born. I'd sit there absorbing every word, not only for the story, but for the comfort of hearing it in his voice again, and I'd admit that his laughter, that deep, rumbling sound that used to fill the corridors, was the only real safety I ever knew.

But the room is empty. The most agonising part of losing him isn't the funeral; it's the Tuesday mornings when I find his old spectacle case. It's the way I accidentally start to dial his number before I remember. It's the culmination that I am now the one who has to check the locks. I am the one who has to be the "roof," but I don't have his strength.

If Nanna were alive, I would tell him that he wasn't just my father. He was my witness. He was the only person in the world who loved the "unpolished" version of me; the version that failed, the version that was scared, the version that didn't have to be "someone" to be loved.

To anyone who still hears that voice in the other room: I am beseeching you, go to him. Don't wait for a milestone. Don't wait for a "talk." Just go sit in the silence with him. Hold his hand while it is still warm. Listen to the story while the breath is still there to tell it.

Because one day, you will be standing in an empty room, staring at an empty chair, learning that **the greatest tragedy of life isn't that we lose them; it's that we only realise what we had once we are left with nothing but the "If."**

Step forward before doubt builds a home in you, before the "If" becomes your only companion.

In Gratitude

Before this book closes, I must return to the true heart of my own story: my Amma. Through every season of change and every shifting tide our family faced, she remained the unhesitant anchor that held our world together. To my Amma, thank you for your inexhaustible resilience. You taught me that true courage isn’t always a roar; often, it is the silent, graceful resolve to keep going when the world feels heavy. You were the one who held the fragments of our lives until they became a whole again, never asking for credit, only ever offering cover from the storm.

Your influence is the invisible thread woven through every word I write and every choice I make. You didn't just witness my life; you gave me the ground to stand on. In your strength, I found my own voice; in your fervid presence, I learned that solidity and stability are daily practices of love. Because of you, I learned to face life not with fear, but with a confidence born from watching yours; a legacy of grace that I will carry long after these pages end.

Letter To Our Readers

To Those Growing Up in This World,

There is something I want to tell you before this book closes, and I want to tell it softly.

By the time we fully understand our parents, life has usually already moved on. We are older then. Busier. More articulate, perhaps. We know bigger words. We know the language of ambition, deadlines, self-care, burnout, distance, independence, and space. We know how to answer emails quickly, scroll without thinking, stay in touch with people we barely know, and disappear from the ones who love us most without even meaning to.

What we do not always know in time is this: love at home often happens peacefully, while we are looking elsewhere.

It happens when someone asks whether we have eaten.

When someone keeps the light on a little longer.

When someone remembers what they like from a particular shop.

When someone waits to hear the gate's sound before sleeping.

When someone notices tiredness in our face before we have found words for it ourselves.

When someone gives advice clumsily, repeats themselves, worries too much, asks too many questions, or says the same thing again and again, not because they want to control our lives, but because their love has nowhere else to go.

When we are young, we think love will announce itself. It will arrive in the form of speeches, celebrations, dramatic confessions, or unforgettable moments. But in most homes, especially in ours, love rarely speaks that way. It becomes routine. It wears ordinary clothes. It sounds like reminders, precautions, practical questions, small preferences remembered, and silent adjustments made in our favour. It does not always know how to be poetic. It simply knows how to stay.

And because it stays, we begin to overlook it.

That is one of the strangest things about being loved deeply. The more constant it is, the more easily we mistake it for background. We assume it will remain where it has always been. We begin to treat presence like infrastructure. We forget that the hands that serve us, protect us, and steady us are not permanent arrangements. They are lives of their own. They get tired. They grow older. They wait. They feel hurt. They miss us in silences we do not see.

It does not tell us when a routine is calmly This is especially true in the age you are growing up in or already living through. There is so much noise now. So much speed. So many interruptions. The mobile phone is always near. The world is always entering the room. Even when we are home, part of us is elsewhere. We are half-reading, half-listening, half-answering, half-living. We tell ourselves we will talk properly later. We will sit with them on Sunday. We will call after this meeting. We will visit when things calm down. We will ask the questions one day. We will listen to the stories another time.

But life does not always announce which conversation was the last relaxed one.

becoming memory.

It does not warn us that one day we will long, with all our heart, for one more ordinary evening we once hurried through.

So this is not only a letter from a daughter. It is also a request to every one who still has time.

Please do not wait for regret to teach you tenderness.

Sometimes sit with your parents without multitasking.

Keep your phone away for a while and let your face be fully turned toward theirs.

Ask them about their childhood.

Ask them what frightened them when they were young.

Ask them what they gave up without speaking of it.

Ask them what kind of people they wanted to become.

Ask them about the roads they took before you were born and the disappointments they swallowed so your life could open wider.

You may be surprised by what you find.

The people you call "Mummy" and "Papa," "Amma" and "Nanna," "Ma" and "Baba," are not only parents. They are entire worlds that existed before you knew how to name the sky. They have carried private fears, unfinished dreams, humiliations, efforts, compromises, prayers, and small victories you may never fully see. And yet, in the middle of all that, they made room for your moods, your mistakes, your becoming.

Value that.

Not in a performative way. Not in one social-media post on Mother's Day or Father's Day. Not in guilt. Not in panic. But in the daily grammar of attention.

Reply with patience.

Listen without rushing.

Notice what they repeat.

Remember what matters to them.

Sit down when they ask you to sit for tea.

Take the extra few minutes.

Go on the drive.

Watch the old film.

Hear the story again.

Let them finish.

Let them feel that their presence still reaches you.

And if your relationship with your parents is not simple, if there are wounds, distances, misunderstandings, or things that cannot be undone, even then, I hope you will carry one thought gently: where love has existed, however imperfectly expressed, try not to let distraction erase what truth remains. Not every relationship can become ideal. But many can become softer. Many can become more honest. Many can still be met with dignity before time closes the door.

If this book has done anything, I hope it has reminded you that life is not made meaningful only by achievements, milestones, and the things the world applauds. Very often, meaning lives elsewhere. It lives in repetition. In presence. In someone thinking of you while buying fruit. In a call asking if you reached safely. In a shared meal. In being known in your smallest habits. In someone loving you faithfully without making a grand performance of it.

That kind of love is easy to miss.

It is also the kind we miss the most when it is gone.

So, before you put this book down and return to your notifications, your schedules, your deadlines, your plans, I hope you pause.

Sit beside someone who once sat awake for you.

Call someone whose love has become so familiar it's gone unnoticed.

Thank them, not because the moment is dramatic, but because it is still available.

That is the miracle.

I repeat: thank them not because it is a special occasion, but because the opportunity is still available. That is the true gift. Not just that you were loved, but that **you still have time to notice.** Once you truly see it, the ordinary will never look ordinary again.

Love,

Sushma

Verses Kindler Publication

Verses Kindler Publication

Reach us through our website -

https://www.verseskindlerpublication.com/

For more information visit our

Instagram or Facebook page

9 789347 494529

Printed at Repro India Ltd.